BEGI … STORY

ROMAN CITIES

Roger Coote

Illustrated by Peter Dennis

Wayland

BEGINNING HISTORY

The Age of Exploration
The American West
Crusaders
Egyptian Farmers
Egyptian Pyramids
Family Life in World War II
Greek Cities
The Gunpowder Plot
Medieval Markets
Norman Castles
Plague and Fire
Roman Cities
Roman Soldiers
Saxon Villages
Tudor Sailors
Tudor Towns
Victorian Children
Victorian Factory Workers
Viking Explorers
Viking Warriors

All words that appear in **bold** are explained in the glossary on page 22.

Series Editor: Rosemary Ashley
Book Editor: Anna Girling
Designer: Helen White

First published in 1990 by Wayland (Publishers) Limited, 61 Western Road,
Hove, East Sussex BN3 1JD

British Library Cataloguing in Publication Data
Coote, Roger
Roman cities.
1. Roman Empire. Cities. Social conditions
I. Title II. Series
307.7′64′0937

HARDBACK ISBN 1-85210-781-2

PAPERBACK ISBN 0-7502-0525-3

Typeset by Kalligraphics Limited, Horley, Surrey.
Printed in Italy by G. Canale & C.S.p.A., Turin.
Bound in Belgium by Casterman, S.A.

CONTENTS

THE ROMAN EMPIRE

The story of Rome started over 2,700 years ago. Some farmers built a small village beside the River Tiber in the country we now call Italy. The village grew into a town and then into a great city – Rome.

Armies were sent out from Rome to **conquer** other lands. These armies were very strong and they defeated almost everyone they fought against. All the lands they conquered became

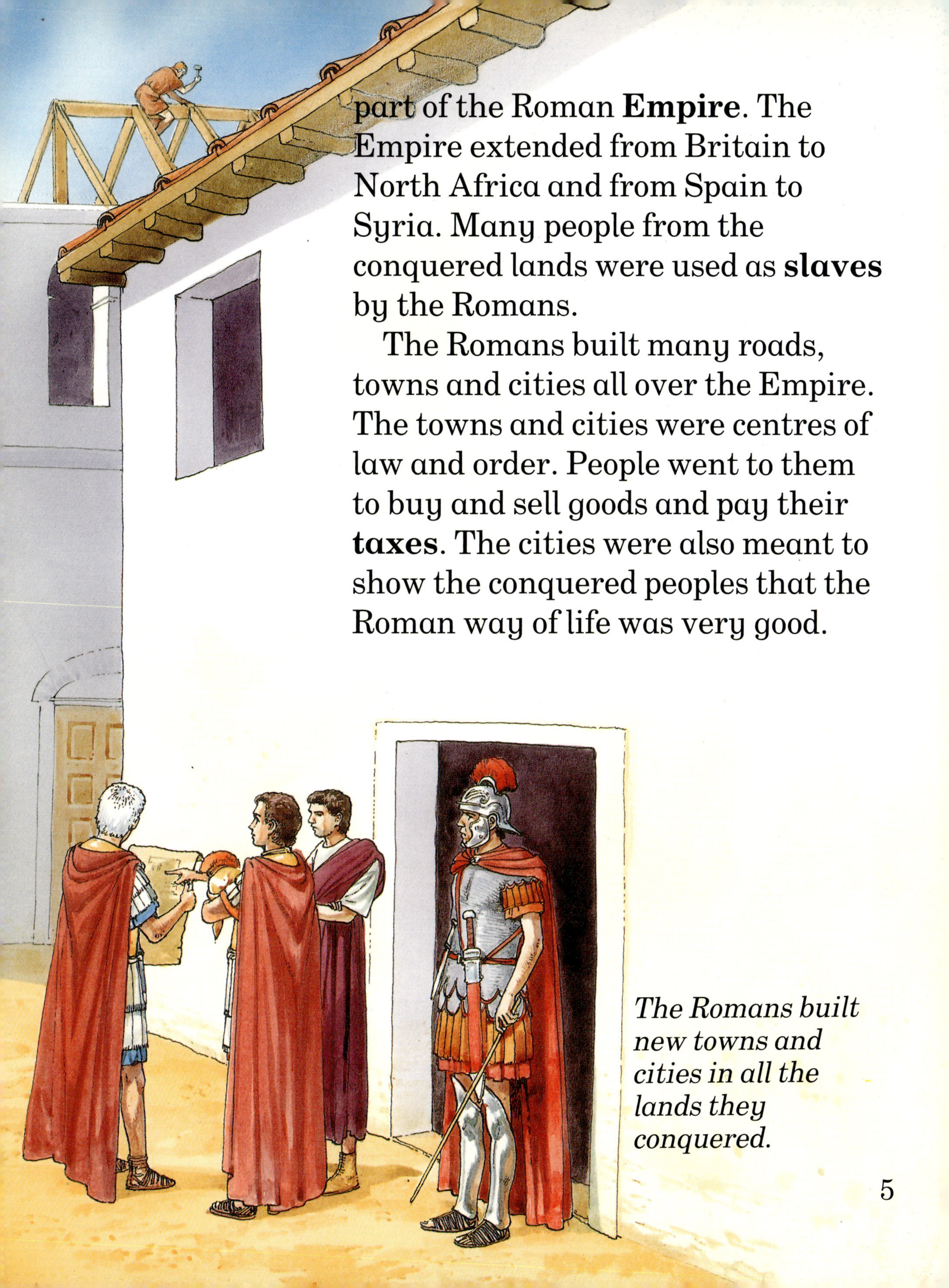

part of the Roman **Empire**. The Empire extended from Britain to North Africa and from Spain to Syria. Many people from the conquered lands were used as **slaves** by the Romans.

The Romans built many roads, towns and cities all over the Empire. The towns and cities were centres of law and order. People went to them to buy and sell goods and pay their **taxes**. The cities were also meant to show the conquered peoples that the Roman way of life was very good.

The Romans built new towns and cities in all the lands they conquered.

The City of Rome

Rome was the centre of the Empire and its largest city. When Rome was at its biggest more than 1,200,000 people lived there. The city was full of grand palaces and houses, temples, theatres and large open squares. Many of the important buildings were covered with a thin layer of **marble**. This made the buildings shine in the sun.

A view over the rooftops of Rome. The large round building is a sports arena called the Colosseum.

There were 85 km of streets and alleys in the city. The main streets were paved and were kept clean. But most of the alleys were muddy and dark. They were also very dirty because people threw all their rubbish into them.

Food for the city came from the farms nearby. Most other supplies came by sea to the large port of Ostia.

THE FORUM

Above *This is the* curia *where the city council of Rome met.*

Below *The ruins of the forum in Pompeii in Italy.*

The forum was one of the most important parts of a Roman city. It was a large open space surrounded by buildings. The forum was often used as a market place. **Traders** set up stalls and sold food, cooking pots and other goods. People also gathered in the forum to talk about the affairs of the city or listen to speeches by the **governor**. There was usually a **shrine** in the forum.

Many important buildings were grouped around the forum. There were law courts where people who had been accused of crimes were judged. The city council met in a building called the *curia*. The *tabularium* was the office where information about the city and its people was kept. Some buildings were offices. In others there were eating houses and public lavatories.

Below *Roman citizens buy food from a stall in the busy forum.*

Above *Some Roman baths had beautiful mosaic floors.*

Below *The city of Bath in Britain is named after its Roman baths.*

THE BATHS

Every Roman city had its public baths where people washed. Some cities had separate baths for men and women. In other cities women went to the baths in the morning and men in the afternoon. People did not go to the baths just to keep clean, but also to talk to their friends, have business meetings or play sports and games.

At the public baths there were several pools at different temperatures. When bathers had undressed they went into a room where they relaxed in a pool of warm

water. Next came a very hot room where there were tubs of steaming water. Soap was unknown in Roman times, so people rubbed their skin with oil and then scraped it clean with a curved metal rod. Finally there was a cold water swimming pool to cool down in.

The water for the baths was heated in big tanks over a **furnace**. Hot air from the furnace flowed under the floor to heat all the rooms.

ROMAN HOUSES

Below *Roman children often played in the* atrium *of the house. In the centre was a pool where rainwater collected.*

Most of the people in a Roman city lived in crowded blocks of flats called *insulae.* If there was a shortage of space for building in the city, more flats were built on top of the blocks, and they grew taller and taller. One block in Rome was so tall that people came from far away to stare at it.

Left *Most Romans lived in blocks of flats like this one, known as the House of Diana in Ostia.*

Rich people lived in large houses with many rooms. The entrance led into a light courtyard called the *atrium*. In the centre was a pool to collect rainwater that fell through an opening in the roof. Around the *atrium* were bedrooms, slaves' rooms, storerooms and a room where guests were entertained. Behind the *atrium* was another courtyard with a garden in the centre. Around it were the kitchen, dining room and lavatory. Some houses had central heating. Rooms were heated by hot air, just as they were at the public baths.

The cooking, cleaning and other work in a Roman house was carried out by slaves.

Below *This mosaic shows a slave at work in a Roman kitchen.*

SHOPS

The streets in a Roman city were lined with shops, **taverns**, eating houses and workshops. Rich people only went shopping to buy expensive things, such as clothes and jewellery. They sent their slaves to buy other goods from the many small shops which sold bread, meat, fruit, vegetables, cloth and so on. The shopkeepers were mostly poor people or slaves who had been set free. The

A tavern selling food and wine, and a shop where people are buying cooking pots and jugs.

taverns sold wine and other drinks, as well as snacks.

Very few homes had kitchens, and so most people went out to eat. They could buy hot meals in take-away food shops. These shops had rows of pots sunk into the counter. Different foods were put in each pot and the pots were kept warm by a fire underneath. Some streets in the city were full of workshops where skilled craftsmen made cloth, shoes, silver items and many other household goods.

ENTERTAINMENT

The Romans enjoyed bloodthirsty entertainments. On public holidays they flocked to **amphitheatres** in cities all over the Empire to watch men and wild animals fighting to the death. First they watched contests between different animals, such as bears attacking buffalos. Then men fought against animals. The most popular part of the show was when

gladiators fought each other with swords, spears, **tridents** and nets. If one man was wounded, the crowd would shout out whether they thought he should be killed by his opponent or allowed to live.

Another favourite entertainment was chariot racing. Races were held at a huge, oval track. The chariots were pulled by two, three or even four horses. The races were fast and dangerous. Many **charioteers** were killed in accidents, but those who won many races became rich and famous.

TEMPLES AND GODS

Below *These people are holding a procession outside a temple.*

The Romans believed in many gods. They thought the gods controlled their lives, and they hoped to bring themselves good luck by pleasing the gods. Each god and goddess had a temple in the city dedicated to them. Only the priests were allowed to enter a temple. The people held processions in the street outside. Animals were

Left *This temple was built in a Roman city in North Africa.*

sometimes **sacrificed** by the priests in the temple.

Jupiter was the most important Roman god. Others included Mars, the god of war, Venus, the goddess of beauty, and Saturn, the god of wine. Some Roman **emperors** were also treated as gods, even while they were alive. People also believed every home was protected by its own gods. Each house had a small shrine where people prayed to these gods.

Below *A shrine inside a house in Pompeii, Italy. This is where the family worshipped their household gods.*

DEFENCES

The Romans built forts throughout their Empire to make sure that the people they had conquered did not rebel. Every Roman town and city also had to protect itself from enemy attack. To do this, each city was completely surrounded by a huge, strong wall. When a new wall was to be built, the first task was to dig a deep trench. Earth from the trench was then piled up and high stone

Below *The walls of Constantinople, now called Istanbul.*

walls were built on both sides of it. When this was finished, the wall was about 3 m thick. It often started below ground level to make it difficult to tunnel under.

Along the top of the wall was a walkway from which soldiers could keep a lookout. There were also towers from which they could shoot arrows and throw spears and stones down on enemies. The only roads into the city were through guarded gatehouses. The gatehouses could be closed when the city was attacked.

Below *From the top of the city wall soldiers could keep watch on the surrounding area.*

Glossary

Amphitheatre A large, circular building where Romans went to watch gladiators fight.

Charioteer A chariot driver.

Conquer To defeat people and take over their land.

Emperor A person who rules over an empire.

Empire A large group of lands which are ruled by one person.

Furnace A fire in an enclosed space which is used to heat water, melt metal or burn rubbish.

Gladiators Men who were made to fight to the death in a Roman amphitheatre.

Governor A person whose job was to rule part of the Roman Empire for the Emperor.

Marble A kind of stone that can be polished to make it shiny.

Sacrifice To kill something to please the gods.

Shrine A small place where gods are worshipped.

Slaves People who are not free to do as they like and are forced to work by a master.

Tavern A shop where alcoholic drinks are sold.

Taxes Money which people have to pay to the ruler of their land.

Trader Someone who buys goods and sells them again to earn money.

Trident A spear with three prongs.

Books To Read

Julius Caesar by Rupert Matthews (Wayland, 1988)

Julius Caesar and the Romans by Robin May (Wayland, 1984)

A Roman Centurion by Stewart Ross (Wayland, 1985)

The Roman Empire and the Dark Ages by Giovanni Caselli (Macdonald, 1981)

A Roman Gladiator by Anne Steel (Wayland, 1988)

See Inside a Roman Town by Jonathan Rutland (Kingfisher, 1986)

Picture acknowledgements

The illustrations in this book were supplied by: C. M. Dixon 8 (top), 10 (top), 13 (top and bottom), 19 (top); Sonia Halliday 8 (bottom), 20; Michael Holford 10 (bottom); Ronald Sheridan 19 (bottom).

INDEX